The Compassionate Psychiatrist

The Compassionate Psychiatrist

Redefining Mental Healthcare

Marcia A. Murphy

RESOURCE *Publications* • Eugene, Oregon

THE COMPASSIONATE PSYCHIATRIST
Redefining Mental Healthcare

Copyright © 2024 Marcia A. Murphy. All rights reserved. Except for brief quotations in critical publications or reviews, no part of this book may be reproduced in any manner without prior written permission from the publisher. Write: Permissions, Wipf and Stock Publishers, 199 W. 8th Ave., Suite 3, Eugene, OR 97401.

Resource Publications
An Imprint of Wipf and Stock Publishers
199 W. 8th Ave., Suite 3
Eugene, OR 97401

www.wipfandstock.com

PAPERBACK ISBN: 979-8-3852-0178-5
HARDCOVER ISBN: 979-8-3852-0179-2
EBOOK ISBN: 979-8-3852-0180-8

VERSION NUMBER 04/26/24

Scripture quotations marked (RSV) are taken from the Holy Bible, Revised Standard Version of the Bible, copyright © 1946, 1952, and 1971 the Division of Christian Education of the National Council of the Churches of Christ in the United States of America. Used by permission. All rights reserved.

This is dedicated to all those
who strive for excellence
in providing care for those
who have mental illness

Our aim must be to help our patient to achieve the highest possible activation of his life.

VIKTOR E. FRANKL, *The Doctor and the Soul: From Psychotherapy to Logotherapy*

Contents

Preface	ix
I. Compassion in Psychiatry: *A Lifeline*	1
II. A Legend: *Kindness in Mental Healthcare*	21
III. Basic Human Rights: *Being Treated Respectfully*	39
Conclusion	51
Bibliography	55

Preface

Exploring clients' ideas and perceptions of compassion and implementing the same in daily practice can be pivotal in redefining mental healthcare.[1]

The secretary directed me through a nearby door into the psychiatrist's office. As I went in the door closed behind me. Dr. [Noyes] stood up from behind a large wooden desk. He was a tall, thin man with fine sandy hair and wire-rim glasses. He walked over, introduced himself, and shook my hand. He had a sophisticated manner though understated, a gentleman of the old world when civilities mattered and were clearly expected. Though he appeared to be in his forties, he seemed older spiritually, a little tired and resigned to his profession's demands. At the time of our meeting I was unaware of the importance this would have for my future, the lifeline it represented.

As we sat down I noticed a Boston fern on the corner of his desk. Staring at its tender leaves I began explaining my unhappiness at being there.

1. Sengupta P and Saxena P, "Art of Compassion," 3.

PREFACE

> "I don't trust you. I don't believe in psychiatry—it was not my idea to come and speak to you."
>
> Unfazed, Dr. [Noyes] began to ask questions.[2]

THIS BOOK ISN'T ABOUT me. It's about those who took care of me for several decades as part of the psychiatry profession. I will only mention my story to keep the narrative coherent. I cannot adequately explain my therapeutic relationship with these physicians unless I include why I had to be seen for treatment. So here is a brief summary.

My mental illness began when I was in my teen years. I was struggling in a family which was full of strife. There, anger was expressed in emotional violence on a regular basis. One of my brothers who suffered from epilepsy, also had severe behavior issues, and threatened my life on more than one occasion. Not feeling safe at home, I joined a quasi-religious cult that took me out of Iowa to other states and big cities like Chicago and New York City. My mental condition deteriorated while practicing the spiritual ways of this cult, the way of prayers focused on a fake Messiah, fasting, and social isolation. The group discarded me in one of its NYC centers when I could no longer fundraise, e.g., selling candles, candy, and flowers on street corners and in businesses. I was living in a cult group residence and became psychotic, hearing terrifying voices for about eighteen months without a break which was devastating.

After about three and a half years I finally left this cult but was a total wreck. I stayed with my parents until

2. Murphy, *Voices in Rain*, 65–66.

after a hospitalization and then the social work system found me a temporary residence in a psychiatric half-way house for women. I continued to receive psychiatric care both as an in-patient and out-patient. I found my own apartment and entered employment though I failed at every job I had. My relationships were bitter failures also. I tried to attend church services on Sundays but lacked transportation so I usually couldn't go. And as I attended weekly Bible studies held close to downtown, the Christians wouldn't give me the time of day, would not offer friendship. My circumstances as an outcast were unbearable and I nearly succeeded in ending my own life.

Fast forward to my writing of many articles and books on the subject of how spirituality is a major factor in recovery from mental illness and how without my faith, I would be dead. I also owe my recovery process to several key figures. Russell Noyes Jr, MD, (hereafter referred to as RN) was one such personality, a physician without whom I would have undoubtedly been homeless, starving, and without hope. Hope, then, is key and RN was the embodiment of hope offered as a sacrifice to heal the wounded soul. He said that God had called him to be a psychiatrist. He touched many lives and I'm grateful to have known him. At one point my mother said to me: "Dr. Noyes adopted you." She meant that as a psychiatric professional he would do his utmost to see that I received the best care. This seemed to be the case because his unwavering and steadfast support helped me through many difficult circumstances for many years. I feel certain that other professionals might have given up. But with RN, I felt protected and safe; that this doctor had integrity and kept his word no matter what. After he retired, I no longer felt safe even though I had a new psychiatrist; but as though I was out in the real world now, all alone. I then found more support in my church.

Psychiatry is extremely challenging for all the healthcare providers who work in this field. RN even told me that he couldn't have done his job without his faith which was what held him up. I'd hate to imagine what other psychiatrists use to cope—maybe alcohol or other such things. Keep in mind that RN was not perfect; however, any imperfections are made small by his enormous integrity and far-reaching vision. Character, then, what a person is made of, becomes evident by the fruit. What does a life leave behind in its wake? I hope to show how a psychiatric professional influenced my life for the better. RN wouldn't allow me to forget the Voice in the Rain, how God's power was made manifest in my time of deep need earlier in my psychotic break (see memoir, *Voices in the Rain: Meaning in Psychosis*). Writing about my past experiences and how faith is important was pivotal in my recovery process, for through the process of writing I was healed.

As a patient or client, however you choose to label those who have a mental illness in a healthcare setting, I offer my experiences and reflections here as a thought exercise for ways to develop a more helpful therapeutic alliance with patients. The scope of the differences in implementing this care depends on a lot of things, each factor specific to the clinical context and setting. Institutions and facilities operate according to their own mission statements in for-profit or nonprofit settings, so this will have an influence in some degree on employee mindsets and work environments.[3]

To describe my perceptions of compassionate care from within the field of psychiatry I've intertwined

---

3. Sengupta P and Saxena P, "Art of Compassion," 3

PREFACE

authentic medical records written by Russell Noyes Jr., MD, with my own reflections upon them. Not all the records are included, just a sampling to give an idea of the scope and extent of the excellent care given by Dr. Noyes. The examples are given to assist the reader in understanding how compassion and kindness make a real difference in a therapeutic relationship which often results in a positive outcome. How patients are treated has a dramatic impact upon the patients' recovery process. Treatment outcome often depends on whether there is humane and sensitive attention given to the patient. Most patients, when their physical needs of food, clothing, and shelter are met are open to receiving counseling assistance. True, some patients may baulk, but loving kindness often wins the day.

I

Compassion in Psychiatry
A Lifeline

Being concerned for the sufferings of others and being motivated to relieve them of their emotional distress, including improving their life circumstances. Taking care of those who need assistance.

A TEAR FELL DOWN his cheek. It appeared that Dr. Noyes could feel the deep tragedy and crisis in my life without me even speaking a word about it. Reaching up with his left hand, he wiped it away then continued with writing a note on a pad of paper. In a chair at the side of the desk where patients normally sit, I viewed Dr. Noyes performing his regular duties as he had now for many years, a professor, employed by a state hospital in a Midwestern city. I had undergone a serious injury and surgery, but had elected not to mention it to him because it was too personal. Instead, I sat tightly wrapped in my beige trench coat, instinctually feeling the need to protect myself and, largely, remained silent. What I did share was how I continued to work on my writing projects and did some research in libraries. Surely, the medical profession had done enough harm already. I didn't want to unnecessarily reveal my feelings or thoughts. My coat gave me a feeling of safety and security along with its tiny lapel pin of a blue cross with surrounding red flames symbolizing the Presbyterian Church (USA).

Being an unusually astute and perceptive counselor Dr. Noyes sensed my coldness, my change of temperament from one in past months of a relaxed, cheerful demeanor, into a rather stiff, business-like composure. Yet, he didn't pry; he didn't try to impose. What he did, though, was provide a presence, someone who respected me as a patient and as a human being, worthy of his time and efforts. I trusted him, but not that much. Some things are simply not discussed.

My surgery was supposed to be corrective, to fix a serious injury that a female physician had caused during an exam in a traumatic clinic appointment in primary care. This injury caused severe, chronic pain for over twenty years that impaired my mobility and general means to function on a daily basis. At the time the injury occurred I pleaded with the doctor for pain medication. She literally laughed in my face and sent me out the door.

I left that clinic for one across town but soon found I was stepping out of the frying pan and into the fire because there was also mistreatment there. Some of the primary care physicians I had were incredible bullies who were not only impatient and unkind but were even overtly belligerent. Medical personnel often think they need protection from mental patients; but, for me, it was the reverse: I needed protection from the doctors and other medical staff.

People say there is stigma being a mental patient; that is absolutely true even in healthcare where all patients are supposed to be treated with respect. I've experienced this stigma in medical care in a blatant and overt manner. I thought: *How can they ignore a conscience which says doctors are in a healing profession?* It appears that people with psychiatric disabilities are considered to be a different species, in an entirely different category all together according to some healthcare professionals: nonhuman, devoid of feelings and immune to physical and/or emotional suffering. This is absolutely false: the mentally ill are probably more susceptible to pain—both physical and emotional—being more sensitive than others.

It is very popular in contemporary times to give credit for the concept of compassion to the Buddhist religion or anything other than Christianity. Christianity is blacklisted. I will not expound in great detail here about why I believe this is misattributed. But I will say that in my religion, my biblical reading gives witness of the ultimate sacrifice of Christ crucified and lays a groundwork for all the rest of my core beliefs, including my own personal worldview. Compassion, then, emanates from a cross. RN carried his cross while working in his field; he gave his all and fought the good fight. It was a blessing to have known him. At one time my life was going in the totally wrong direction. He helped me get back on track to walk the narrow road.

PROGRESS NOTE

January 6, 1995

Marcia says she is getting along satisfactorily. She has ups and downs. She is taking risperidone 1 mg twice daily and trazodone 100 mg at h.s [hour of sleep]. She does not report side effects with this combination and seems quite pleased with it. It seems to her that she sleeps well. She reports that her religious life is growing increasingly important to her and that it is a source of considerable strength. In an essay about her experience she credits risperidone and her religious faith with her improvement over the past year. And it would seem to me that these factors are as she says all important. She has been doing more writing I think lately and she has been sharing some

of it with me, and I do believe she has some talent for expressing herself. I have encouraged her in that regard. I've suggested continuing the same dose of medication. We reviewed some of her thinking about an attitude toward her illness and some of her volunteer activities. I am suggesting that the medication remain the same and that she return in 2–3 months.
—Russell Noyes Jr, MD

My life was stormy, so RN's influence as a counselor and doctor provided something stable that I could count on. Seeing him every few months gave me some stability. As he mentioned in this note, my return to my childhood faith further strengthened me. I had been brought up in a church but the experience in the cult and the psychotic break had pretty much destroyed my ability to believe. When he asked me if I believed in God at an earlier appointment, I remarked: "I want to; but I can't."

RN respected my intelligence and encouraged me to independently experiment with the dosage amounts of my medications and then report back to him. I was the one who experienced the effects of various amounts of medication, so he trusted me to decide how much to take. He also gave me permission to phone him when I felt the need and he always took the time to answer or return my phone calls. The manner in which he communicated with me was always pleasant, kind, and with empathy. His tone of voice was always caring and concerned. Some doctors think they have to brutally dominate and control the patient. RN was never like that.

This accessibility for reaching RN in my early years of treatment was pivotal for me regaining a foothold in life. His constant willingness to assist me for many years was foundational in my recovery process and I will always be grateful.

PROGRESS NOTE

June 30, 1995

Marcia says she is getting along better and has found a solution to her problem with depression and stopped taking Effexor that I had prescribed a few weeks ago when she phoned about being depressed. She is part of the Stephen's Ministry Program at [the church she attends.] She has been volunteering at the Mental Health Center Day Program and feels that she is contributing by offering social support. She has been varying doses of risperidone and trazodone. She has had a little more difficulty lately with some nightmares, however. Marcia certainly looks good today, looks relaxed and smiles easily. I suggested continuing medication at the current dose but also, sometimes, she could experiment with the dose because I think it may be helpful for her to learn what these medications can and cannot do. The higher dose of risperidone we had her on initially had seemed to contribute to depression or lack of motivation. She discovered that one day when she had forgotten to take her medication and started feeling much better. Since the time she had that experience, she has maintained a lower dose of the medication daily. She will return in three months. I have been seeing her on a three-monthly basis and she phones me from time to time.
　—Russell Noyes Jr, MD

Unfortunately, RN's impressions: "Marcia certainly looks good, looks relaxed and smiles easily," was only cosmetic. I was suffering a lot and did not have the outward appearance revealing my painful condition. Over the years, hospital staff and others have not really known my real condition because I have made a big effort to take care of my outward appearance by bathing daily, wearing clean clothes, and acting appropriately. Sharing my internal suffering wasn't in my skill set. Only when I began to write about my feelings and people read my writing could anyone know of my depth of suffering. But until I did the writing, people judged me by my neat outward appearance and they thought everything was fine, including RN. One thing, though, that comforted me and allowed me to genuinely smile was being in RN's presence during appointments. For brief moments I felt happy.

PROGRESS NOTE

October 5, 1995

Marcia looks quite good and has a bright smile. In terms of medication, she is taking risperidone 1 mg in the morning and 3 mg at night, and trazodone 150 mg at bedtime. She has cut down on her use of caffeine considerably. Marcia has been doing quite a bit of reading and has found her concentration better. She prays a good deal and one of the things she prays about is that she not be so impulsive. At any rate, she looks quite well and appears to be doing very well indeed.

—Russell Noyes Jr, MD

I. A LIFELINE

I did well for a short time, probably a few months, but then went into a difficult period; I found it difficult to function, as described in the following note.

PROGRESS NOTE

March 14, 1996

Marcia said she is not doing quite so well these days. She finds it hard to keep up with keeping her apartment clean, she doesn't exercise, doesn't go out much. Marcia decided that trazodone, which had seemed to help her sleep for a while, had been causing her to have bad dreams and she discontinued it. The trouble sleeping is less, she says, because she has reduced her intake of caffeine considerably. She doesn't use any caffeine after noon and she believes this was much of the problem before. However, she used the caffeine in order to stimulate and motivate her and may be having some let-down from not having that available now. She describes her mood as low sometimes and that she cries, and I said anti-depressants are available and depression is not something she should put up with.
—Russell Noyes Jr, MD

I know RN was trying to help, but depression is more than biological; it is something that has a psychological, environmental/social, and spiritual source, with biological in connection. We needed to try to find the root causes of my distress. I would feel down for a while, then find some inspiration again, pick myself up, and go forward for a little while. The following note describes my on-going mental conflict with social problems and how it relates to the church.

THE COMPASSIONATE PSYCHIATRIST

PROGRESS NOTE

May 10, 1996

Marcia reports that she is getting along satisfactorily. She is taking 4mg of Risperdal. She is planning to join a Presbyterian Church. She said she is dealing with feelings about conflicts in some of her relationships. I told her that she should consult with the minister and try to set these conflicts aside. As I said to her in part, it is an imperfect world and one really can't resolve all conflicts or ambivalent feelings, and one really shouldn't always be trying to do so.
—Russell Noyes Jr, MD

During treatment with RN, I brought up some concerns related to my relationships and teachings of the church. Since I was involved with a church, I questioned whether having a boyfriend was sinful, to put it bluntly. Marriage was not possible due to financial problems. Because I was on disability benefits marriage wasn't an option because the benefits would be greatly reduced if we got married, and the benefits would be reduced so severely we would find it difficult to survive. So, RN told me to talk to my pastor about it. At the time there was an interim associate female pastor and I met with her. She said I was not sinning because the circumstances would not permit a sanctioned formal marriage and I shouldn't worry about it. But she also said that the problem of acceptance in the church would always be there, it would never go away. I also went by what Dr. Noyes advised: *It is an imperfect world and one really can't resolve all conflicts or ambivalent feelings, and one really shouldn't always be trying to do so.*

I. A LIFELINE

PROGRESS NOTE

July 18, 1996

Marcia reports that she is doing well. She just had an item that she wrote accepted for publication in the academic journal, Schizophrenia Bulletin, and is quite pleased. She has signed up for a program to assist her with employment. She is wondering at this time if she might be able to handle something on a part-time basis to supplement her income. She notes however, that if she earns $200, she is only able to keep $50 of it because the government would reduce her disability payments accordingly, as well as the housing assistance program lowering the amount of her rental assistance because of her increased income. So, the incentive is not great. However, she wishes to be as productive a citizen as she is capable of. And it seems to her that now that she is doing things especially well that she should test herself in this regard again. Marcia continues to publish a newsletter for the Mental Health Center Clubhouse Program. She showed me copies of the newsletter and they looked quite professional. Marcia offers no complaints today. She does not report distress. I will continue to see Marcia about every other month and she phones from time to time. I am recommending that she continue with the present medication.
—Russell Noyes Jr, MD

There were no incentives for paid employment which in my case really amounted to slave labor because of low wages and my benefits cut back. I never was able to come out ahead. If I had a college degree, this could have helped; however, I only had twelve months of formal college education so was only able to obtain entry-level positions which did not pay much. No matter how much I tried, I could not come out ahead financially: could not afford to pay for rent, food, clothing, or other necessities. Government policies punish the disabled who try to break out of poverty. There was just no way out in my case.

PROGRESS NOTE

August 30, 1996

Marcia phoned and wondered if the weakness she has been experiencing might be related to risperidone 3 mg daily. She says she has a hard time standing, has to drag herself around, and is shaky and weak. She has not mentioned this to me previously but it sounds as though she might be having a little parkinsonism related to the drug. I said we might try a lower dose (such as 2 mg daily), but said we might also want to try Cogentin to see if that would counteract this. It is sometimes difficult to separate some degree of apathy or lack of motivation, negative symptoms of schizophrenia from drug-induced symptoms or depression. Her preference is to reduce the dose, as she said she is tired of taking drugs and hates to add a new one which would have its own side effects. I said let's try reducing the dose and see what that does first.
—Russell Noyes Jr, MD

Later in life, I developed symptoms of weakness along with severe pain in all parts of my lower limbs: cramping, shooting, stabbing pain—every kind of pain you could list—in my legs, ankles, and feet: muscles, joints, and every part of limbs. These symptoms progressed in severity and are identical to Primary Progressive Multiple

Sclerosis (ppMS). The doctors I saw in Neurology did medical gaslighting. I was female and wasn't listened to. I also wasn't important enough as a psychiatric patient on Medicaid to be given a major diagnosis even though my symptoms fit the criteria for ppMS. One neurologist only wanted me to be a subject in an EMG lab, and when I declined, he wouldn't help me further. I repeat, they wouldn't listen to me.

On several occasions when I was waiting for an elevator at the hospital while doing my volunteer job, I lost strength and had to lean against a wall. Another time, when I was doing research at a big library, I was standing waiting for an elevator, and totally lost strength and, exasperated, cried out loud to nobody in particular: *I can't do this!* I then started to use a cane. My condition deteriorated from use of a cane, to using one crutch, to two crutches, to a wheelchair. Sometimes, I would fall down. Other times, I wasn't strong enough to do home chores. Eventually, I acquired a home health aide. My psychiatrist was the only medical professional who did believe me and encouraged me to try to get help with an evaluation at the Mayo Clinic. However, Mayo would not do an evaluation. Again, discrimination.

PROGRESS NOTE

September 12, 1996

Marcia reports that she is having problems with lack of motivation and also with depressed mood, negative thoughts, and so on. She says that it is difficult living alone, that she is lonely. She has substantial financial problems due to being without Section 8 housing assistance for now

and is on the waiting list to restart in this program. She had to go off Section 8 when she lived with her boyfriend and now the wait is a year-long before she reaches the top of the wait list. Her family and relatives will not assist her in any way: not with clothing, food, or other basic needs. The neglect is severe. Marcia is desperate and struggles to survive. Thus, the depressed mood. Even though she attends church worship services weekly she struggles, also, to retain hope, hope in the future and for her basic needs. She says that sometimes she thinks she would be better off dead and has even asked God in prayer for God to kill her.
—Russell Noyes Jr, MD

The previous note is self-explanatory. Poverty could be worse than the mental illness because you can't even find enough resources to survive on on a day-to-day basis. My family was always big on saying the words: "I love you!" but there was not any real evidence of this; they did very little to help me survive. The one exception was my sister who sometimes purchased clothing for me, and made a down payment on an apartment. She was the only one who occasionally assisted me.

PROGRESS NOTE

November 7, 1996

Marcia has been having kind of a tough time lately. She has been having some depressive symptoms, has felt little motivation, and has felt isolated. She repeats to me that her financial difficulties have undermined her, and have made her feel like her family and others don't care about her. Her boyfriend won't give her any assistance and her

I. A LIFELINE

father has never provided assistance. She feels her mother reacts negatively about money because her mother also has financial problems. Marcia looks forward to obtaining housing assistance in a month or two, which will be a considerable help to her in this regard. Marcia doesn't have much motivation and doesn't do much in her own apartment. She uses quite a bit of caffeine early in the day to get herself going. She avoids caffeine in the afternoon so that won't interfere with sleep at night. Her mood gets low. At one time she had signed up for a program that would allow her to test herself out in the workplace but now she feels so depressed that that makes it impossible; so she has decided not to go through with it (which I agree with). She will return for follow-up in two months. Commonly, she contacts me by phone about one thing or another, usually medication adjustments in between times.

—Russell Noyes Jr, MD

I would do well for a while, then fall back into depression. I latched on to coffee, sweets, a new friend, and finally, the church. Being part of a religious community was a big, major improvement. I now found more inspiration for writing. RN said to me at the same time: *Remember the Voice in the Rain and all that means to you and all that brought about.* For the reader who is unfamiliar with the Voice in the Rain, please refer back to my first publication: *Voices in the Rain: Meaning in Psychosis, a memoir.* For me to remember this meant: How does religious faith have an impact on the quality of my life? How is my religious faith foundational to my recovery process? And with any new developments and achievements I must give the credit to God who is the healer and sustainer. Without God, I am nothing.

THE COMPASSIONATE PSYCHIATRIST

My main focus was to teach others that spiritual exercises of church attendance, daily prayer, and scripture reading would vastly improve mental health. People who have mental illness need to take some responsibility for their own mental health. Sure, we still need doctors, and friends, socializing, etc. However, as human beings and creatures, we were created to be in relationship with our Creator. Ignoring our Higher Power, turning our backs on God, simply, and plainly, is not a good idea; it won't work.

So, let's look at compassion at a deeper level. How can a mental health professional have compassion? Does compassion exist inherently from within the human being since birth? Is it an intrinsic quality instilled in some mysterious way without our conscious awareness? Are we born that way? Or is it all learned from the environmental input and rewarded by extrinsic methods such as with the gold stars in elementary school: do well and we are rewarded. Some people believe that healthcare professionals need monetary rewards for being kind to patients as measured in surveys. I think that is absurd. Kindness, though thought to be essential for healing and good health outcomes, should not be bought and sold like a gold brick commodity. Instead, we need to encourage staff to think of a golden rule: *How would you, yourself, feel in the patient's position? How would you want to be treated?*

So, ultimately, one pertinent issue among many, that needs to be addressed is: Can compassion be taught, e.g., the lesson of the golden rule. Can a person learn to be sensitive to the needs and feelings of others? What made RN different from all the other professionals in the clinic? Why did he stand out? Do psychiatrists *learn* to be compassionate? Does our medical school curriculum though created by the most brilliant minds in medicine really

1. A LIFELINE

have an impact on the students' hearts as it addresses the topic of empathy? *There is soft science taught in medical school and much emphasis on compassion and empathy.*[1]

But what do the students in the end really come away with? Are they just going through the motions and simulations without these things having a permanent, long-lasting impact on them? Or do people, instead, need the hard, painful lessons learned only in their own personal experiences, *the school of life,* that would possibly soften their hearts? Many wise men have said that we become compassionate only because we, ourselves, have suffered in a similar manner. If this is, indeed, the case, then a young, enthusiastic, and emotionally squeaky-clean medical student who has not been exposed to much so far in life, may lack the disposition to really care about suffering human beings. It may take some time. But if compassion and empathy really can be taught, then that's a whole different ball game.

Religious institutions radically assume that good values like compassion, can be taught. We see this in Sunday School lessons and activities for children and sermons preached on the topic for adult congregants. It would make things a whole lot easier if we, personally, did not need to suffer in order to be concerned with the suffering of others and thereby take steps to provide them relief from distress. Maybe it depends on how sensitive a person's constitution is. Are they empathically aware of other's feelings? Do they feel the emotions of others when physically close to them or even when spatially not in the same proximity? If so, then the despair and hopelessness that other people experience is sort of an emotional contagion, and it spreads spiritually, nonmaterially, and

1. Peg Nopoulos MD, Chair, email to author, 12/29/2023.

through walls, in a sense. One need not be physically present to feel the pain of hopelessness. That war on the other side of the globe with people being bombed and killed mercilessly? Some people can feel that. The disasters all around us can be crushing in on us. So much violence and bloodshed, we can feel all of that. No wonder masses of people are depressed and lose hope. No wonder, people have anxiety. Perhaps only those who have their minds focused on some other-worldly goals can tolerate the vibrations of a vast mass of suffering humanity.

The church I attend has continuing adult education in their Learning Academy on topics like empathy. Perhaps this is what healthcare professionals also need in the hospital/clinics setting: continuing education and refresher courses on how to provide compassionate care. Many, I feel, lose touch with their nurturing selves as they are immersed in the fast pace of care delivery and computers, forgetting to be kind to their patients. Perhaps, if they are required by the administration to brush up on topics pertaining to good attitudes and kind mindsets in treatment delivery their patients would benefit and heal. A caring attitude cannot be faked. Patients see through the hard-hearted doctor who puts on an act. What we need are genuine, thoughtful individuals who are in the field with the intent to facilitate and promote healing.

Unfortunately, I have come across psychiatrists who would have made a better choice of employment in law enforcement as their personalities match that of a police officer. These individuals who call themselves doctors have absolutely no comprehension of a healing model for psychiatric illness. It is all *control, control, control: power and control.* With this type of insensitive, on-going treatment patients do not stand a chance for recovery. The patients do not have a caring provider; only someone with a prison warden-type personality who tries to manipulate them with judgmental and harsh tones of voice, mannerisms, and facial expressions. These psychiatrists mistook the medical field of psychiatry for the Department of Corrections. They think their primary role is to condemn the patient and keep them in line. As a result, patients are disrespected and boundaries in therapeutic interpersonal relations are dissolved, the patient loses autonomy, their privacy is destroyed, and they are made to feel small and insignificant. Nothing they do is ever good enough; there are never any rewards or acknowledgments of successful achievements. They are always criticized and made to feel unwelcome in the department.

RN was different than that. He and I partnered in the belief that medications were important, but he also suggested ways for me to think that allowed reflection on the meaning and purpose for my life which added more psychological depth. This meaning was sufficient to keep me going during dark times. After a near-fatal suicide attempt at the age of thirty-nine and a recovery period, I spent time reflecting on RN's questions which included the following points:

1. What meaning has serious mental illness had for you?

2. How have you been able to find this meaning and what has it meant in terms of recovery?

3. What attitude have you taken toward the suffering it has caused?

4. What has been the mission of your writing, your responsibility? Having had the experience (you know what it's like), you can say what things helped and can help others.

THE COMPASSIONATE PSYCHIATRIST

Our previous focus, before my suicide attempt, had been largely on medicine and a somewhat superficial accounting of my daily activities and social life. It seems that was all there was time for. What I found post-suicide attempt was that I hungered for the psychological answers and theological basis for recovery. It became apparent that psychology and theology belonged together as cofactors in the recovery process, this in addition to medication management. Let there be no mistake: I was grateful for the medication; however, alone, it would not provide the holistic recovery sought after. All three factors were to be the basis of recovery: biological, psychological, and theological. And with this came social reintegration, acceptance, and friendships. Productivity was an additional gain, resulting in meaningful work and contributions to society as a whole. RN, as a caring and sensitive guide, supported my efforts to find this deeper meaning.

11

A Legend
Kindness in Mental Healthcare

Russ Noyes is a legend in our department. My entire career, including residency, has been at Iowa so I have had the pleasure to work with Dr. Noyes over the years. I came to appreciate the kind of clinician he was, and the kind of person. I heard somebody characterize him as "both the tortoise and the hare." He was somewhat slow, yet it was in the context of always being contemplative. He was also—at the same time—an incredibly quick wit with keen perception. The most salient feature of his character, however, was his kind and gentle nature, and his compassion for patients. He had a warm soul and a golden heart.

Peg Nopoulos, MD
Paul W. Penningroth Chair of Psychiatry
DEO, Department of Psychiatry
University of Iowa Carver College of Medicine

Marcia has a bright *smile*.

Dr. Noyes made a note in the medical record.

Dr. Noyes retired.

Marcia made a note: I never had a bright smile again.

Though our relationship was purely a professional and therapeutic one, my reliance on him as a type of mentor and support was tremendous. Even now, my impulse on many occasions is, *I need to ask Dr. Noyes about that!* Or *I need his opinion and will send him an email*—and then I realize I can't because *he's gone*.

PROGRESS NOTE

June 5, 1997

Marcia reports that she is getting along satisfactorily; but some things are stressful; for example, her father and stepmother are in town for the summer and she says that often her father is a difficult person and she tries not to be around him very much. He will sometimes come across as self-centered and pushy and shows no concern for her difficulties like her struggles to obtain basic needs such as food and adequate clothing. Another thing that's stressful is that she feels out of place at Bible study at times because everyone seems so at ease and relaxed and she doesn't so

this puts stress on her. She is taking 4 mg daily of risperidone and says it gives her a feeling of greater emotional stability. She finds she is less impulsive, that she doesn't feel driven to throw herself into activity. She stopped taking Serzone and expresses the opinion that it might be a dangerous drug because she had the feeling of things snapping in her brain. Also, she said that when she took trazodone for sleep it caused her to have nightmares and that disappeared as soon as she stopped taking it. I see her about every two months and today she brings with her proofs [publisher's copies of her manuscript] of an article that has been accepted for publication in the academic journal, the *Schizophrenia Bulletin*. I think it is a fine piece and it will be published in August. I think this is something she can be proud of.
—Russell Noyes Jr, MD

RN always supported my writing and research for projects. He would encourage me on a regular basis. I needed that. Facing, daily, the struggles with my chronic illness and the harsh reality of stigmatization from my relatives and the community, I would often grow discouraged. The rejection by relatives and people in the surrounding culture was almost too much to bear. Writing alone in a library, back in a secluded area, gave me some kind of protection and allowed me to pour out my thoughts and feelings in prose. But I don't really know much about how my publications have had an impact as many readers did not provide feedback. There are a few who have responded by saying my writing is helpful; but they were few and far between.

II. KINDNESS IN MENTAL HEALTHCARE

PROGRESS NOTE

August 7, 1997

Marcia said she has an article coming out in the *Schizophrenia Bulletin* and is looking forward to that. I continue to feel that she has done much better since being on risperidone; however, during this same period of time she has also had a strengthening of her religious faith. It also may be that risperidone has some antidepressant properties. She is active in writing and editing a newsletter for the Mental Health Center Clubhouse. She looks well today, smiles easily. She is not very spontaneous but certainly is logical in conversation. There is slight blunting of affect [facial expression shows little emotion]. There is now a slight reduction in spontaneity and of course she continues to describe a fluctuating lack of motivation and initiative. She also describes some difficulty in concentration. I continue to see her on a regular basis every two to three months. Today, I am recommending no change in medication.
—Russell Noyes Jr, MD

RN frequently mentioned the importance of my faith in my recovery process in his medical records. I told him that and he agreed. Getting involved in a church had its ups and downs. The stigma of being a mental patient existed in my church experience. Early on, most people wanted to stay away from me. Some acted very frightened of me and would clutch their small children close to their bodies in fear. I wanted to say to them: I hope I'm one of the good ones: I read my Bible and pray every morning. I come to worship God on Sundays. I won't hurt you; I love you. I just want to be your friend.

THE COMPASSIONATE PSYCHIATRIST
PROGRESS NOTE
November 6, 1997

Marcia is getting along satisfactorily. She continues to take 3 mg risperidone at bedtime. She has obtained a computer for word processing and is doing some writing. She has taken a leave of absence from the Mental Health Center Clubhouse newsletter. She said that going there was causing her some distress because some men would harass her. She thought that she would not go there for a while. She wrote me an interesting letter about a presentation a psychiatrist did at her church for their Adult Education program. She gave me some things she had written and also showed me some responses she had received from her article in the *Schizophrenia Bulletin*. I told her that she had received a greater number of responses than I had ever gotten. I continue to encourage her to write and said I will look over or make suggestions on anything she does if she would like for me to. I have been seeing her every two months and suggested continuing that in the same interval. In between times she calls sometimes to report depressive symptoms and wonders about taking an antidepressant. This has been very much an off-and-on kind of thing and it is sometimes difficult to distinguish between negative symptoms of schizophrenia, loneliness, and genuine depressive symptoms.
—Russell Noyes Jr, MD

    I bought a used computer and printer and hooked it together, the cables, etc., myself, without written instructions. This brought my writing to a new, higher level. I still wasn't on the internet, but writing became a daily habit. I was thrilled with the new technology. It was an

IBM compatible desk top computer. When I asked RN for his suggestions or direction for an article, he provided this cheerfully. This kind of on-going assistance was pivotal for my success in publications. Gradually, I attended workshops on the college campus and in surrounding cities; this, too, helped to educate me on the methodologies for literary writing. At one point, I received writing instruction from graduates of the University of Iowa Writers' Workshop. RN always advised me to write about my own experiences with mental illness and my recovery process. As a part of that, I chose to describe the importance of faith in recovery which was the foundation or bedrock for improvement in my health.

PROGRESS NOTE

January 12, 1998

Today Marcia showed me an article she had written for the *Psychiatric Rehabilitation Journal* describing her experience with stigma and that of other mentally ill persons. I feel that it is very well done and likely to be accepted for publication. In fact, I suggested there might be more she could do along these lines. I suggested seeing what there is in the literature on the subject of stigma, particularly personal experience of such stigma. I thought Marcia looked quite good today. Her mood seemed normal. She smiled easily. She continues to take 3 mg risperidone. I am not aware of side effects she is having with this drug. I continue to see her once every other month.
 —Russell Noye Jr, MD

THE COMPASSIONATE PSYCHIATRIST

As RN mentioned, the problem of stigma is very powerful. Because of stigma, there is less funding allocated for programs to aid and assist the mentally ill. Even in medicine, the general clinics, the mentally ill are sometimes treated in a substandard way, verbally abused, and as in my case, also physically abused. For some unknown reason, physicians will forget their manners and sense of courtesy with psychiatric patients. The doctors will forget that these are real human beings who require care and kindness. Granted, some patients may come across as belligerent; but usually, it is in the minority. When we get to the root of the problem, we find that some mentally ill are used to inhumane treatment and so they are reacting in anger. However, once a person is treated with kindness and respect, they will respond with respect also. It has to go both ways.

I will describe something I witnessed in a psychiatric clinic waiting room: a psychiatrist came in and called a patient's name. He was a Black man and he got up to go with her. The first thing she said was: "Hi, how are you? Oh! That's a nice watch!" And then, "*Where did you get it!*" the doctor demanded to know in an accusatory tone. I saw that as a person of color, his wrist watch or jewelry was under suspicion immediately as though he was a shoplifter This disrespectful attack on his character was not only inappropriate for a greeting; but especially not appropriate spoken loudly in a public space, the clinic waiting room, where he would be humiliated because other people in the room would hear the doctor's accusation. Such lack of respect is probably uncommon, generally speaking, in psychiatry. But this one day it seemed to stand out as both, unusual and damaging behavior.

II. KINDNESS IN MENTAL HEALTHCARE

PROGRESS NOTE

May 14, 1998

Marcia is continuing to take risperidone 3 mg daily and she looks good, smiles easily, and seems relaxed. She says her church involvement is rewarding. She says there is some concern she might have initial stages of diabetes and this might need to be controlled with diet. She indicates her mood is satisfactory but her motivation is not very high. She volunteers at church by serving coffee on Sunday morning, participates in a Bible study on Wednesdays, and assists with the church newsletter. She reports that another of her writings has been accepted for publication in a book that will be distributed to congregations about the experience of living with chronic illness and the religious aspects of this. She seems to be doing satisfactorily with risperidone and I see no real reason to change to a different antipsychotic medication. She will return in 2 months.
—Russell Noyes Jr. MD

Gradually, the church volunteer work increased my social integration. I was cautious and found social interaction a challenge. I didn't know what to say to new people. They always asked personal questions and I usually had to reveal that I had a psychiatric disability. Stigma would immediately follow with some individuals rejecting me and others keeping their distance. Though I was in the Bible study for approximately twelve years I failed to make one friend there who was my own age.

THE COMPASSIONATE PSYCHIATRIST

PROGRESS NOTE

July 20, 1998

Marcia is doing satisfactorily but reports she has developed type II diabetes. She wants to control it with diet so has lost ten pounds. Also, because of hypothyroidism she is taking a supplement and her energy has improved a little. Her residual schizophrenia manifests itself in low motivation, energy, and lack of interest, but she continues to benefit from risperidone 3 mg. One thing that captures her interest is her religious faith and her participation in her church is very meaningful. I see her every two months and advise no change in medication.
—Russell Noyes Jr, MD

RN, being a man of integrity, went to get lengths to show respect for patients. Once I was sitting in the psych clinic waiting room for an appointment. After a few minutes past the scheduled time, RN came out in his long, white physician's coat and said to me: "Marcia, I apologize. Something's come up and it's going to be a while before I can see you for the appointment. Why don't you go have a cup of coffee. It may take some time before our appointment. I will see you as soon as possible. Again, I apologize for the wait."

PROGRESS NOTE

September 24, 1998

Marcia looked real good today. She sent me an article she wrote and I thought it was a good one and I complimented her. She commented that when she feels depressed, she thinks its situational and this last time made a list of situational things. They included missing a lot of church Bible study because they don't meet during the summer and prayer groups don't always meet. It's nice to hear her feeling this sense of belonging and missing activities of that kind; but her point was that perhaps she needs to pay a little more attention to factors and how to cope with them rather than using medicine. The article that she wrote expressed a fairly strong sense of purpose and belonging through her belief in God and her religious community. I think she is doing rather well.

—Russell Noyes Jr, MD

Early in my interactions with the organized church down a few blocks from my home I could really feel how different a Christian social environment was compared to the outside world. True, I didn't make any close friends early on; however, the relationships, which varied in depth, were some things I was clinging to for dear life. At times, my thoughts were that I needed to stay alive one more week and go to Sunday worship service. I just need to get to church on Sunday and Wednesday Bible study. I need to bathe. I have to wash my hair. I need to pray. I need to go there down the block again. My goal was to not kill myself, to live long enough to make it to another worship service on Sunday. And then the next. And the next.

PROGRESS NOTE

March 12, 1999

Marcia reports that she has times of being depressed, experiencing loneliness and isolation. She feels best when

she is writing she reports to me, and she has certainly some success in publishing pieces of her experience of illness. I have encouraged her to keep writing. She takes risperidone 3 mg daily. She remains active in her church and is preparing a presentation for a Bible study despite initial trepidation about doing so. I think Marcia looks good and she smiles brightly. She brought with her today two things she has published about which she is rightfully proud. I told her that I had bought and read the book that she had recommended about writing. An excellent book. I continue to see her every two to three months and she calls from time to time about problems that arise but I am not really doing much these days.
—Russell Noyes Jr, MD

RN was steadfast in his support of things that mattered to me. Writing was a healing activity. Bible study, another healing factor. Doing the first presentation for the Bible study group was a major turning point. I did the preparation with trepidation. I was very scared to be up in front of the group. This kind of thing was foreign to me. As it turns out, years later, I did presentations for the UI Carver College of Medicine and the College of Nursing, along with various churches and other organizations. Giving talks for medical students, with PowerPoint slideshows, the students gave me the rating of 4.95 out of 5 according to what the director told me.

II. KINDNESS IN MENTAL HEALTHCARE

PROGRESS NOTE

May 7, 1999

Marcia says she has been doing well and poorly. She indicated that she got really excited about a book that I mentioned to her but then when she finished reading it, she had a let-down. She reports some trouble sleeping and has limited her caffeine intake and feels this helps. She has diabetes now and feels her occasional low blood sugar may contribute to feelings of depression. She tells me that she needs to be out on a regular basis, out of her apartment and be interacting with people or she gets lonely. She continues to have a lot of interest in writing. She is thinking about taking on a book-length project, which I've encouraged her to do, and I feel she is capable of doing. She wondered about seeing her medical record and if it was available to her. She told me about a project she has done interviewing people with psychosis and she is planning to write up the results of these interviews that focus on the meaning of psychosis for people who have experienced them. She continues to take risperidone 3mg daily and I continue to see her every two months.
—Russell Noyes Jr., MD

A psychiatrist who offers sympathetic support to a patient will get far greater results than a psychiatrist who is constantly critical, negative, and judging. A psychiatrist who shows interest in supporting a patient's efforts to be productive, however small, will find greater results. The problem with two-week in-patient stays (dictated by insurance), is that there is only emergency care and not a sustained support system upon discharge. Upon release from the hospital, the lack of care is tragic because the patient will not have the social means to heal psychologically. Without on-going care, a patient may fall back into old destructive habits and behaviors which will result in re-hospitalization, the revolving door phenomenon. This is especially true for the homeless population and those with addictions.

PROGRESS NOTE

July 7, 1999

Marcia reports that she is getting along satisfactorily. She has continued to do some writing about severe mental illness and its relationship to religious faith. She did a project in which she interviewed several persons who had experienced psychotic episodes and who report that their spiritual lives have been affected by the psychosis. I think it is well done and I have encouraged her to find a suitable publisher. It disturbs her that sometimes she is not working and sometimes she wonders what she might be capable of. I think that even though she continues to do relatively well, full time work would be a challenge for her that she might not be able to meet and part-time work offers no incentive. Whatever she gains in income, she loses in housing and disability benefits. I do not, in fact, think she is capable of sustaining employment. For example, she phoned a few weeks ago and said that revising a manuscript according to the requirements of a particular journal had overwhelmed her and I suggested that she set the project aside for a few days. She is taking 2mg risperidone for a while to see if she has more energy. She continues to struggle with some negative symptoms, some lack of initiative, and motivation at times. She does not report to me

II. KINDNESS IN MENTAL HEALTHCARE

positive symptoms [hallucinations] recently. I continue to see her every two months.

—Russell Noye Jr., MD

Even though I was not well enough to sustain paid employment, RN did support the writing projects because that was all I was capable of doing for a while. It's important for psychiatric patients to have financial resources through disability benefits or family, so they have some basic needs met; and this will then allow them to pursue work on a volunteer basis. Being somewhat productive gives a person with mental illness some stability and structure to their day. And it will help someone to feel that their life is worthwhile.

PROGRESS NOTE

November 4, 1999

Marcia reports that she is getting along satisfactorily back on 3mg risperidone daily. We discussed her recent activities including writing a book. She reports that her religious faith is most important in her life. She continues to attend regular Bible study and church services and has friends among the congregation. She continues to struggle with lack of motivation and negative symptoms, including the feeling of emptiness at times and lack of interest. She struggles to keep going with her writing projects. She struggles with her self-esteem which is affected by her inability to work. She wishes she were able to work, but she has tested this many times. Mood seems to be good at present. She brought in a number of questions today but no outstanding problems. She should continue risperidone at the same dose and return as usual in two months.

—Russell Noyes Jr., MD

I started to write a full-length memoir about my life experience with mental illness. This was a project that I focused on for many years. At first, everything was new to me and I had a lot to learn. Along the way, I met other writers and teachers who would shape my authorship. My first published article in a professional journal in 1997 was the beginning of my Mental Health Initiatives church ministry program (MHI). These resources were eventually posted on my own personal website, https://hopeforrecovery.com/, and are evidence and support for an integrated approach to psychiatric care in treating the body, mind, and spirit. Through my writing I explain how spirituality, alongside of biology and other factors, is an integral part of recovery and is essential for healing the emotional, psychological, and physical suffering inherent in illness. Research has shown that spirituality in particular or, religious faith, play an important role in the recovery process.

PROGRESS NOTE

February 17, 2000

Marcia seems to be doing well although she has been working on a book and as she writes about her experience in the cult it causes her much sadness and depression so she cannot do a lot of writing at one time. She continues to take risperidone 3mg daily and we talked about decreasing the dose to 2mg because of tiredness it causes her. However,

she thinks that on 2mg she is likely to sleep less well and I suggested to her that she talk to a pharmacist about obtaining a pill cutter and try a dose of 2.5mg at bedtime. We talked a good deal about her writing and she is getting another article published, something she is quite proud of. She thinks of the book she is writing is giving her life some meaning which I think it does and is a worthy project. I think she writes well and should be pleased with the success she has had with publishing some articles. I think she is doing a nice job with this and I want to encourage her in any way that I can. Today, she seemed in relatively good spirits. She might show a little blunting of the affect, a little diminished spontaneity, but her thinking seems normal. She reports no hallucinations, although I did not specifically inquire about this. Complaints are usually those of negative symptoms, lack of motivation, difficulty sustaining effort and interest and so on. I will continue to see her on an every other month basis.
—Russell Noyes Jr., MD

When reviewing the previous note, I am struck by how kind and supportive RN is. He really knew how to find my strengths and encouraged me to use them over a sustained period of time. This was crucial to my recovery process.

III

Basic Human Rights
Being Treated Respectfully

Treat others the way you want to be treated.
Don't do anything to someone that you
wouldn't want done to you. Put yourself in
another's place. How would you feel?

I'LL BE THE FIRST to admit that I don't always treat others respectfully. I sometimes fail. But I try to monitor myself and improve over time. I think I make an effort. I just ask that psychiatrists do the same. I know that doctors and staff get burnt out. They can be overworked, carry a heavy load, and be exhausted, both physically and emotionally. They have time constraints, deadlines, and have to deal with the insurance companies and pharmacies. Many factors enter in and fuses can be short. Just dealing with various kinds of patients can also be a major challenge.

PROGRESS NOTE

April 13, 2000

Marcia reports that she is getting along satisfactorily. She tells me that she has reduced her dose of risperidone to 1mg because at 3mg it may have reduced her alertness and made her thinking less clear. She thinks that with a lesser dose she is clearer and has more energy. Today she expressed doubts whether she suffers from a mental illness or is she simply a victim of a traumatic childhood and emotional abuse at the hands of the cult she joined for a time. She wonders what may appear to be negative symptoms might simply be the result of stigmatization. Marcia seemed serious and sensitive and there is a slight blunting of her affect. Some reduction in spontaneity. She does not report hearing voices although this may occur off and on. I see no paranoid tendency in her thinking but rather at times a marked sensitivity. I consider her diagnosis as one of schizophrenia. Although it is uncertain whether she ever experienced true delusions. Negative symptoms are the most bothersome including the lack of motivation, apathy, lack of spontaneity, and reduced interest. I told her I felt that a low dose of an antipsychotic helps to provide stability. Perhaps even some reduction of negative symptoms. I think she has done the best that I have seen her since she has started taking risperidone. She points out her religious faith has been important and I agree with that certainly. I suggested she return in two months.

—Russell Noyes Jr., MD

The above note shows that RN was indeed a medical doctor and knew all the signs and symptoms of mental illness, specifically schizophrenia. He also had some idea of what depressive illness was, lack of motivation, and reduced interest, etc. These latter symptoms have remained with me my entire adult life. It must have been difficult for RN to deal with this because these problems were constant. It is significant that he never gave up and showed a tremendous amount of patience.

PROGRESS NOTE

November 2, 2000

Marcia is a patient I have followed for many years who suffers from residual schizophrenia. She currently takes risperidone 3mg daily. She suffers from significant negative symptoms including lack of motivation, diminished interest and initiative, reduced spontaneity. She also at times suffers from social isolation, loneliness, and demoralization. When I use the term *demoralization,* I am referring to a lack of hope. She is significantly bolstered by her religious faith and her participation in a local congregation. She is currently writing a book about her lifetime experience of mental illness and the spiritual meaning that she found in psychosis. She is getting along satisfactorily with risperidone. I think since she has taken it she has done significantly better than beforehand. She has few side effects except for weight gain. She has never been delusional but has suffered from auditory hallucinations.

—Russell Noyes Jr., MD

A couple of years after RN wrote the above note he retired. He found another faculty member to take over my case. The change was dramatic. With a new psychiatrist I quickly learned that each psychiatrist has their own style, temperament, and personality. Some are easy to get along with and others are more of a challenge. With Dr. Noyes, my orientation for recovery was more solitary, working in libraries alone, reading and taking notes, creating articles and books; sending emails to editors and publishers and others in the psychiatric field. So it came as a shock to my system that upon the recommendation of my new psychiatrist I began to do volunteer work in a very busy hospital. If Dr. Noyes was my doctor for solitary, literary work, then this new psychiatrist was providing opportunities for social interactions. It wasn't easy and I had a lot to learn. Beginning this kind of volunteer work at the age of forty-nine I was a bit of a late bloomer. That just goes to show how severe and life-long the traumatic effects of schizophrenia and clinical depression were in my case.

Even though I had a new psychiatrist, RN's early influence continued to have an effect after his retirement. Even though I worked as a volunteer I kept working on new writing projects at the same time based on earlier themes and, as I touched upon earlier, eventually became a public speaker, first, to psychiatric nurses, and then for medical students, church groups, and the general public. I felt I had gained from RN a sense of mission and motivation to share what I called, my message. RN never imposed his own set of religious beliefs on me, but he felt it important to encourage me to explore my own spirituality. And when I voluntarily shared with him that I was brought up in the Lutheran denomination and had visited other kinds of Christian organizations over the years, he gave positive encouragement. It is well documented in the literature, especially in my former writing, that spirituality and religious practices can be healing factors in mental health. If I had had an atheist psychiatrist who did not support me in my spiritual quest, my life's direction could have been very different. I'm not saying it's impossible for an atheist therapist to do well with patients; however, it's been my experience that differences in the moral outlook and perspectives can be troublesome. I'll just say that Providence brought RN and I together and my life's trajectory headed toward the light; but I acknowledge that there were a few bumps in the road.

RN knew from a relatively young age, his twenties, that he wanted to be in a healing profession in service to the mentally ill. RN gave me permission to share his essay he wrote for his church newsletter. I include it here in full to provide a glimpse into his thinking on the topic. For the reader who is not religious, it can be seen from the social activist perspective of altruism:

> When I was a senior medical student, God called me to become a psychiatrist. At the time, I could not have said what attracted me to the field, but looking back, I think I was drawn to the mystery and intellectual challenge it presented. In addition, I recognized in myself a feeling for mentally ill people that could be important in understanding and working with them. Then too, I saw that they were often demoralized if not stigmatized and that for them I could be an advocate.
>
> When Jesus asked the [sick] man at Bethesda if he wished to be healed, he replied, "Sir, I have no man to put me into the pool when the water is troubled, and while I am going another steps down before me" (John 5:7 RSV). His words convey the alienation and helpless resignation often experienced by those with severe mental disorders. Many, in addition to illness, face overwhelming circumstances, and like the lepers of Jesus' day, know the disapproval of their families and communities. But, the mentally ill of this world are part of God's creation. They are children of God, created in His image, and mindful of this I strive to show them the respect and concern they are due. If healing occurs, it is by the grace of God. Medication and therapy are His instruments.
>
> I have been fortunate to see great progress in the field of psychiatry over my forty-year career. Effective treatments have been developed for what were once thought to be untreatable conditions. This has meant that lives have been changed and the stigma attached to illness has lessened. I thank God for the opportunity he

> has given me to witness and share in these advances. I am also grateful for the opportunity I have had to serve these people in need. Through the years I have gained increasing respect for those who struggle with mental illness. Their view of the world enriches us and their courage gives us strength. And, their faith in the face of hardship glorifies God.[2]

It is a very rare occurrence to find one human being caring about the welfare of another human being. It just doesn't happen very often in my part of the world even in the healthcare setting. RN told me that for a lot of psychiatrists it's just a job, employment, a means to an end: status, vacations, travel, accumulation of wealth. Sometimes mistreatment may occur if the doctor is personally having a bad day. I had a negative experience with one psychiatrist, I won't mention names: After RN retired, several years later, I had been at the ER because I had suicidal thoughts. Upon release from the ER, the psychiatrist there told me to do a follow-up phone call to another psychiatrist within a few days of being released from the ER. So, following instructions, I did just that. But when I phoned this psychiatrist and told him I was told to do this and why, he sounded very angry like he didn't want to be interrupted—which I totally understand. His attitude and tone of voice was very deprecating, harsh, and cruel. In this brief encounter it appeared that there wasn't enough time for him to attempt to understand my situation or why I had had suicidal thoughts. It was clear to me that phoning him wasn't a good idea. I had been following directions but as a result was treated badly. I lived for the next few weeks feeling unsupported.

---

2. Noyes, "A Reflection on Stewardship," CTK newsletter.

III. BEING TREATED RESPECTFULLY

RN didn't pry into my personal life. He left it up to me as to what to disclose. I could talk about whatever I was comfortable with at appointments. He never asked me about my personal life. I did decide to share some things with him, but there was never any pressure. He respected me as an adult and left the choices for discussion up to me. He properly kept boundaries and didn't try to control me. I always felt that he saw me as a grown up and not someone to toy with. He was never a bully or someone trying to get his own way. He was a gentleman in the truest sense.

As I previously mentioned, there was a psychiatrist who seemed to lack social skills; either that, or he was just plain rude at times. It is possible he was brought up in a different culture where it was acceptable to act like this and others also acted this way. At one point, I did mention to this doctor that I had a lawyer. I didn't say it was for any problem with him, but he became more kind for a little while anyway. I've come to believe that in Iowa, which ranks last in the nation with just two psychiatric beds available for every 100,000 residents (as of 2024),[3] the psychiatric professionals who *are* available are overworked, over-extended, and burnt out because of the heavy work load, so much so, that some may become demoralized and cease to be civil on some occasions. Anyway, I'm giving them the benefit of the doubt.

Still, there can be problems because at times some doctors/psychiatrists think they own you. They think you owe it to them to disclose your most private matters and when you don't, they give you a hard time. They are wrong. How would these psychiatrists feel if someone tried to intrude into their own personal and private lives?

3. Ramm, "Iowa Worst," para 3.

THE COMPASSIONATE PSYCHIATRIST

I'm sure they wouldn't like it. They need to put themselves in the patients' place and treat them accordingly, with respect and boundaries, not bullying to try to obtain personal information—which is none of their business anyway. Patients deserve their privacy just like everybody else. Once there was a different situation where a psychiatrist prescribed a medication that caused weight gain as a side effect; and then, when I started to gain weight he got angry at me for gaining weight, and blamed it all on me.

As I briefly mentioned in Part One, I began to experience weakness in my lower limbs and RN made a note of this in the medical record in the mid-1990s. I am mentioning this subject again because I was denied the right to good medical treatment regarding this and I want to stress the point. Gradually, as time went on, I also started to have increased pain in both of my lower extremities that is now severe, crippling, and restricts my mobility. Several years after RN retired, when I first let a psychiatrist know about this at an appointment, there was absolutely no compassion. This doctor made it clear that he didn't want to hear about pain by his facial expression, tone of voice, and dismissal of the problem. I know some people go into medicine for the money, prestige, vacations, and trips. I overheard a couple of young residents enthusiastically discuss their vacation plans when I was standing, waiting for an elevator in the hospital. It is possible that some good doctors will fail to provide compassionate care because they are over-worked and burnt out. They may recognize that patients are often in pain, are seeking help, and depend on them. However, when a psychiatrist is tired, perhaps having a bad day, they are unable to provide adequate care. Maybe the psychiatrist has a headache or his research article has been rejected.

III. BEING TREATED RESPECTFULLY

Whatever the reason, I guess sometimes psychiatrists are just unable to show concern. I'm sure there are other times when they will show compassion.

Because of its effect on how I feel daily and the extent of disability, I came to believe through my research that I have Primary Progressive Multiple Sclerosis (ppMS). The doctors I sought help from did medical gaslighting, as I touched upon earlier. The poor or low-income population, female gender, those on Medicaid, as well as those with a psychiatric diagnosis, are not respected or listened to, and are the least likely to be given a total work-up and are not given a major diagnosis and no follow-up care either. I know that my progressing pain and weakness, along with other significant symptoms directly point to ppMS. This is a deteriorating condition. When I later shared with RN this information in email, he immediately voiced concern and sympathy, saying he read the ppMS webpage I shared with him on-line and he hoped it would not progress too quickly and not be too severe. RN always respected my intelligence and point of view.

In the proceeding months after Dr. Noyes passed away (physically died), I was a little semi-psychotic and the summer heat didn't help. I cannot tolerate high temperatures and get semi-psychotic then, also. My writing projects displayed a chaotic disorder. At first, I was disappointed that he retired and then I got angry at him for dying. How dare he give up and abandon me? I soon realized that he did not give up, but that aging and the frailties that accompany that were the inevitable outcome for us all, and I needed to have patience. *We are mortal.*

I did feel comfortable sharing with RN through email about a new friendship I developed with a homeless man I had met downtown soon before RN died. When I

THE COMPASSIONATE PSYCHIATRIST

told RN a few months before he passed away that I had a new relationship with a homeless man he immediately, along with his wife, gave his blessing when responding in an email. They said they were very happy for us and they believed that the relationship had great potential. RN said that he and his wife would pray for us that our needs could be met.

Right down to the end of RN's life, he treated me with kind regard and when he planned his memorial service before he died, he listed me as one of the four speakers at this funeral. The family wanted me to speak first before his three adult children. When the minister called me up front, I made my way to the podium, limping with one crutch. I read from two publications my descriptions of interactions with RN. One was from my first encounter when I was in my twenties, and the other one was of the last appointment, when I was in my late forties. As I read the excerpts I felt the Holy Spirit come upon me. I also felt Dr. Noyes was there. I struggled to hold back the tears. Even now, at the end of his life, he held me up in his funeral and gave me this honor to speak in his church before those present from the psychiatric department, to all those who knew what an extraordinary human being he was. He wanted me to speak about faith, not giving up, and remaining strong in the face of adversity. Even to the end he cared about me, proclaiming to the world what mattered most in our therapeutic relationship.

Conclusion

Russell Noyes Jr. led by example. He didn't preach or boss people around. He quietly did his duties with determination and skill. However, he paid a great price. With lack of adequate funding from local, state, and federal levels, there are fewer resources available to help the mentally ill. With fewer staff and facilities, the resulting enormous client workload on the existing staff can become almost unbearable. With fewer providers and facilities, the psychiatric healthcare providers in place can get burnt out, so much so that some may be unable to provide humane care. For some, with their own needs of rest and recuperation not being met, interactions and communications with their patients are sometimes strained or of poor quality. And sometimes, communication is diminished or practically nonexistent.

I've personally witnessed psychiatrists go from being strong, loving, and kind providers to being exhausted, stressed out, and weary human beings. Excessive exertion and lack of sleep takes its toll. Some psychiatrists lose faith in the medication and doubt research-based therapies. Often, a patient will be the one to bolster up the doctor when they say how great their antipsychotic medication makes them feel.

THE COMPASSIONATE PSYCHIATRIST

Just like patients, healthcare providers can also lose hope. Some turn to alcohol or other means to try to gain a foothold. RN had his religion. But it was more than religion; it was a powerful faith in God. Now Dr. Noyes is gone. We need new blood, new, young doctors who love a challenge and see psychiatry as a door to new, exciting opportunities and adventure. Maybe the research in the field would excite the medical student who can then take a leap into mental healthcare to pursue new treatments.

I hope all those who remember Russell Noyes Jr will carry on his work with courage, boldness, and conviction. He would be pleased to know this.

> Doctor [Noyes] and I walked down the hall to his office. As usual, he walked beside me. Some psychiatrists go ahead of the patient, which is not wrong; yet, Dr. [Noyes] was always at my side physically and, metaphorically, as a means of support. I had not always appreciated this stoic friend; in fact, once I had even run away. Having misunderstood something he said, in a childish tantrum, I vowed to never return. I stayed away for two years. But when I came back, I found him still willing to support me in desperate times—times of confusion, stupidities, and utter despair.
>
> Now at this last meeting it was hard for me to grasp the fact that I had to say good-bye. What is this profession where relationships must follow strict rules of *objectivity?* Dr. [Noyes] had broken those rules because he sincerely cared about my condition and had gone far beyond the call of duty, often sacrificing his own comfort and peace of mind . . .
>
> Over the years, whether I acknowledged it or not, [Dr. Noyes] was the lifeline that kept

III. CONCLUSION

me from homelessness, starvation, and total starvation . . .

Doctor [Noyes] straightened in his chair; he then leaned forward and even though I avoided his eyes I felt them focused on my face. His voice became stern almost to the point of anger, yet I knew he was not angry.

"Don't give up," he said slowly, and after a slight pause, "Don't give up."[4]

---

4. Murphy, *Collected Writings*, 109, 110, 112.

Bibliography

Murphy, Marcia A. *The Collected Writings of Marcia A. Murphy: Christus Magnus Medicus Sanat* (Christ, the Great Physician, Heals). Eugene: Resource. 2020.

———. *Voices in the Rain: Meaning in Psychosis.* Eugene: Wipf & Stock. 2018.

Noyes Jr, Russell. "A Reflection on Stewardship," *An Essay originally published in newsletter of Christ the King Lutheran Church.* Iowa City, Iowa, 2000.

Ramm, Michaela. Iowa Worst in the Nation for State Psychiatric Beds, Report Says. How a New Plan May Help. Des Moines Register. January 24, 2024. https://www.desmoinesregister.com/story/news/health/2024/01/24/new-report-shows-iowas-critical-shortage-of-state-psychiatric-beds-legislature-reynolds/72312936007/

Sengupta, Pramita & Saxena, Priya. "The Art of Compassion in Mental Healthcare for All: Back to the Basics." Indian Journal of Psychological Medicine. 2023, 0(0) 1–6.

www.ingramcontent.com/pod-product-compliance
Lightning Source LLC
Chambersburg PA
CBHW071752040426
42446CB00012B/2528